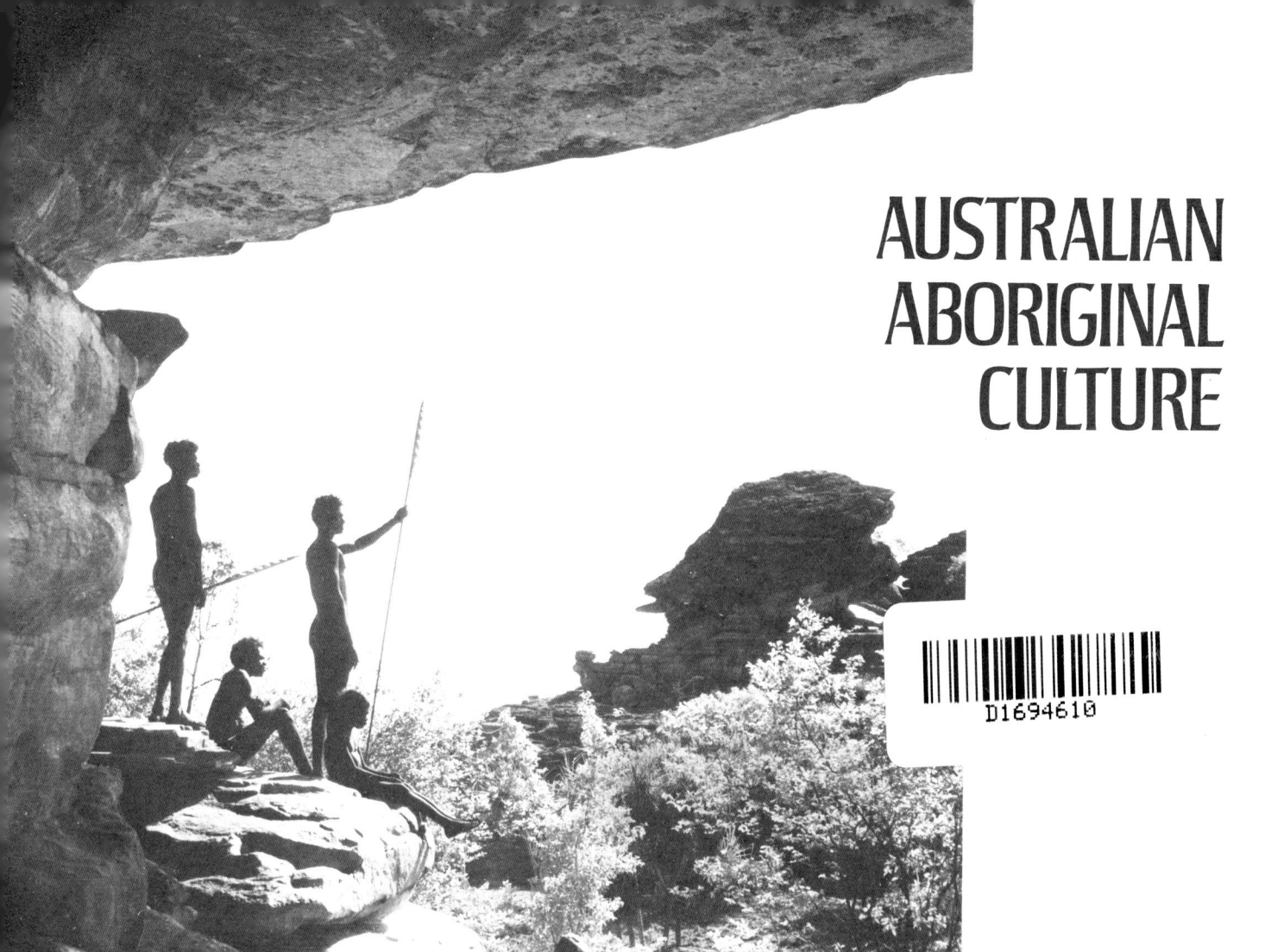

AUSTRALIAN ABORIGINAL CULTURE

Contents

Preface *1*
Who are the Aboriginals? *2*
Aboriginal origins *4*
Tribal lands *6*
The men's way of life *8*
The women's way of life *10*
Dwellings *12*
Fire making *14*
Religion and ceremonies *16*
Magic and medicine *18*
Games and music *20*
Dress and ornament *22*
Watercraft *24*
Hunting and fighting *26*
The boomerang *28*
Material possessions *30*
Stone tools *32*
Bone artifacts *34*
Trade and exchange *36*
Rock engravings *38*
Cave paintings *40*
Bark paintings *42*
Old age and death *44*
What of the future? *46*

Preface

The Unesco General Conference in 1949 decided to promote the mutual understanding of the peoples of the world by exchange of cultural exhibitions prepared by Member States. In accordance with this resolution, the Australian Unesco Committee for Museums decided to prepare for the first time a comprehensive travelling exhibition on the way of life of the Australian Aboriginals.

Funds for the project were allocated by the Australian Government through the National Commission for Unesco whose Committee for Museums set up a working party consisting of Dr A. B. Walkom (Director, Australian Museum) as Chairman, Mr F. D. McCarthy (Curator of Anthropology, Australian Museum), and Dr N. B. Tindale (Ethnologist, South Australian Museum) to plan and prepare the display. It was assembled at the Australian Museum over a period of three years, and most of the work of selecting and arranging the specimens, photographs and art work and of preparing the text of the brochure, was carried out by the then Curator of Anthropology, Mr McCarthy.

The exhibition toured Australia, New Zealand, United States and Canada. It was disbanded and the specimens returned to the State Museums from which they had been borrowed. Over 100,000 copies of the brochure have been sold. It has proved to be so popular and useful, particularly to school children of all ages and to the layman, that the Australian National Commission for Unesco decided to issue a completely new edition. Mr Robert Edwards, Deputy Principal of the Australian Institute of Aboriginal Studies, has prepared the revision.

Several major steps have been taken by the Australian Government in regard to the Aboriginals. One was to set up the Australian Institute of Aboriginal Studies in December 1961 to promote research on the people and their traditional customs. The Institute has financed many hundreds of studies on their human biology, social and economic life, languages, music, art, religion and prehistory; it has made a number of films of their crafts, daily life and ceremonies, built up an archive of several thousand tapes of their languages and music, and compiled a vast bibliography of the knowledge recorded about the Aboriginals.

The other steps taken were to establish the Department of Aboriginal Affairs, the National Aboriginal Consultative Committee and the Aboriginal Arts Board. These bodies co-operate with State and other agencies in the improvement of Aboriginal welfare, health, education and in the promotion of arts and cultures.

The radiocarbon method of establishing the age of camp sites of Aboriginals has demonstrated that their ancestors arrived in Australia at least 30,000 years ago, and indications are that they came long before. When the forebears of the Australian Aboriginals in ancient times sailed across the sea lanes separating Australia from South-East Asia they became the first known navigators. Prehistorians have excavated in Australia the most ancient human cremation and edge-ground stone axe-heads known in the world. This remarkable people, after almost two centuries of contact with the white man's civilisation, is now seeking to establish its own racial image and identity and to preserve as much as it can of its languages, beliefs and ceremonial sites.

F. D. McCarthy

Who are The Aboriginals?

The Aboriginals are the indigenous people of Australia; their origin is uncertain although it is generally accepted that they came to Australia from South East Asia by way of Indonesia. Some scientists see Australoid elements in parts of southern India, Malaysia and especially New Guinea.

The Aboriginals are typically of medium height, with slender limbs, heavy eyebrows, deep-set brown eyes, wide nostrils, a long head and a somewhat protruding lower face. Pigmentation ranges from light tan to dark brown and almost black, while hair is dark brown and grades from straight through wavy to curly.

In common with other continental populations the Aboriginals adapted over many thousands of years to a wide range of environments. The people of the colder climates of southern Victoria and Tasmania tended to be short and thick-set, an adaptive development which would help to conserve body heat, while at the other extreme, in the hot central deserts, the typical build was taller and lean.

The Aboriginals entered a continent that had few diseases. Although mammals were present in Australia the great majority were marsupials, whose diseases were not transmittable to man. Introduction of diseases through centuries of intermittent contact with Indonesian trepang fishermen, especially Macassarese from the island of Sulawesi (Celebes), and later and more significantly European settlers, had a profound effect upon the indigenous Australians. Following European settlement, thousands died of smallpox, venereal disease, tuberculosis, whooping cough, measles, leprosy and influenza.

Since coming to the continent more than 30,000 years ago the Aboriginals lived as hunting and food gathering people, until forced to adapt to European ways. Strong bones and teeth were probably the result of a genetic factor supported by a natural nutritious diet. Older people often had worn teeth from chewing fibres to make them pliable and ready for rope-making and due to the large quantity of sand and grit in their food. Dental decay was almost certainly unknown until the introduction of Western foods such as sugar and flour.

The social **organisation** of the Aboriginals classified individuals and codified behaviour by kinship, age, family, clan and local groupings. Tribes were usually subdivided into two groups and again into four or eight sections. Members of a clan, sub-group or section could not intermarry.

Religion linked the people, their land and nature through the ancestral beings, the pre-existence and re-incarnation of spirits, totemism, mythology and ritual.

The Australians had considerable cultural diversity and expressed themselves aesthetically through a rich heritage of art and a wealth of songs, music and verbal 'literature'.

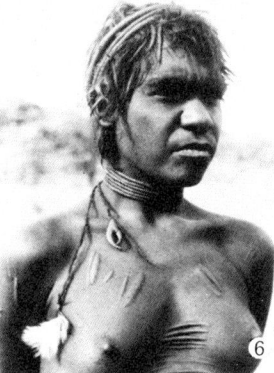

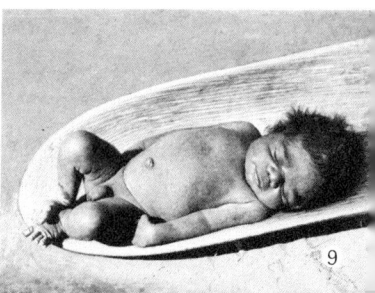

1 - Aboriginal family, MacDonnell Range, Central Australia.
2, 3, 4 - Three generations of a western desert group.
5 - The younger generation.
6 - Young Aranda woman.
7 - Blood-wood seeds used as a decoration.
8 - Aboriginal of the central desert. 9 - Baby in 'cradle'.

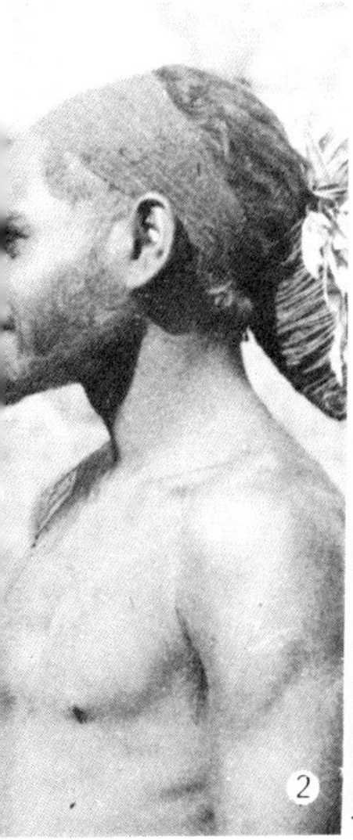

Aboriginal Origins

Access to the Australian continent was relatively easy during the last great Ice Age when much of the earth's water was locked up in massive ice sheets stretching over the whole of Canada, northern Europe and vast regions in the Antarctic so that ocean levels dropped dramatically. There were times when the sea was at least sixty to ninety metres lower than it is at present. During these times of extreme low sea level Java, Sumatra and Borneo were part of the Asian mainland; this was separated from the combined Australia-New Guinea continent by water gaps of less than 160 kilometres and perhaps little more than 100 kilometres. People with some form of watercraft made their way to the great southern continent. This crossing to Australia by the Aboriginals at least 30,000 years ago is the earliest evidence of sea travel by prehistoric men.

Some 15,000 years ago the ice sheets began to melt as a result of a gradual rise in temperatures throughout the world. About 10,000 years ago the sea had risen to within fifty-three metres of its present level to separate Tasmania, Kangaroo Island and other offshore Australian islands from the mainland. The people inhabiting Tasmania became isolated and developed physical and cultural traits of their own. As the sea level rose still further New Guinea was cut off with the formation of Torres Strait and the present Australian coastline was established about 5,000 years ago.

The first people to reach Australia found it a favourable environment, probably with conditions generally better than they are today. Besides present day fauna there were numbers of giant animals, now extinct, which were an added source of food. These included the rhinoceros-sized *Diprotodon* and *Procoptodon* a three metre high kangaroo. The dingo was not native to Australia, but came as a companion pet with some of the later arrivals. Excavated dingo remains found in the South East of South Australia are dated to about 8,000 years ago and as dingoes were not present in Tasmania or on Kangaroo Island when Europeans arrived it may be inferred that the dog was brought to the continent about 8,000 to 10,000 years ago.

The precise characteristics of the first Australians are unknown. So too are the chain of events that resulted in the modern Aboriginals. They could be the product of a mixture of physical types which entered the continent at different times or of a single people with a wide gene pool who made a variety of adaptations to produce an extended range of physical characteristics.

Archaeologists and anthropologists seek answers to these questions by studying ancient mineralized human skeletons found at a number of widely separated sites including Talgai in Queensland, Keilor near Melbourne, Cohuna and Kow Swamp in northern Victoria, Tartanga and Roonka in South Australia and at the Lake Mungo and Lake Nitchie sites in western New South Wales. The Mungo remains are about 26,000 years old. Continued study of such sites, and of the excavated bones themselves, is certain to produce important information about the origins and physical history of the Aboriginals.

1 - Australia at the time of low sea level during the ice age. The sea level on this map represents a lowering of the sea by 200 metres. Although during the Pleistocene epoch sea level rarely dropped to this depth, the nature of the sea floor contours are such that dry land normally approximated this outline.

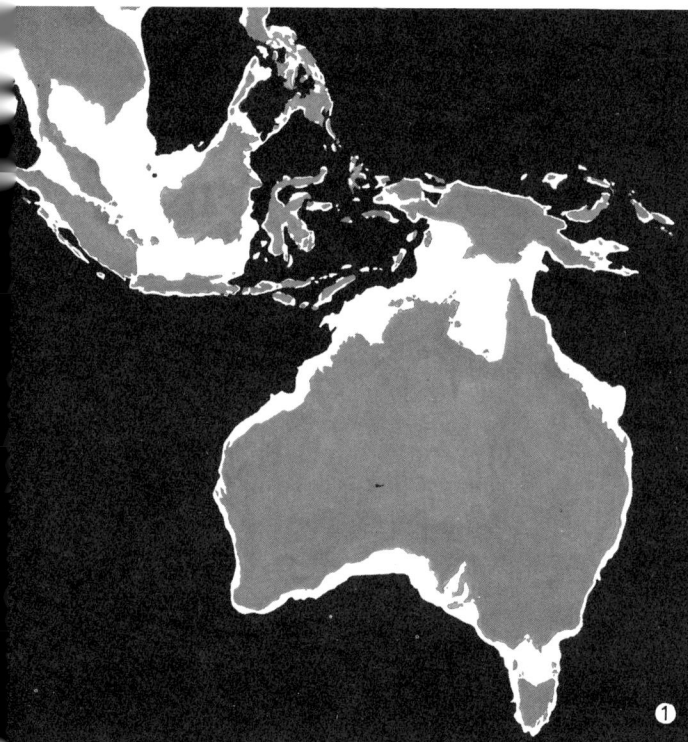

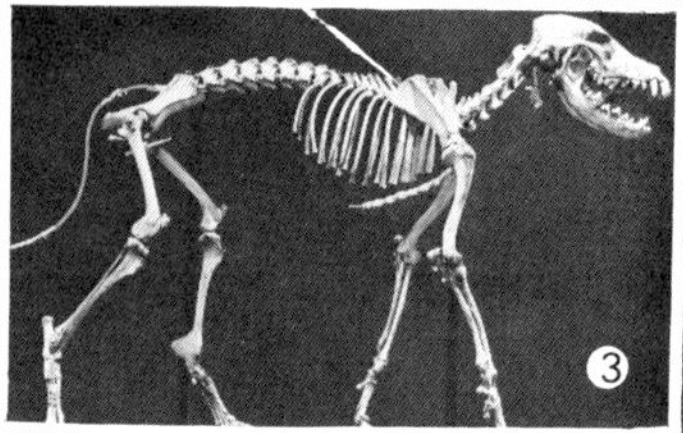

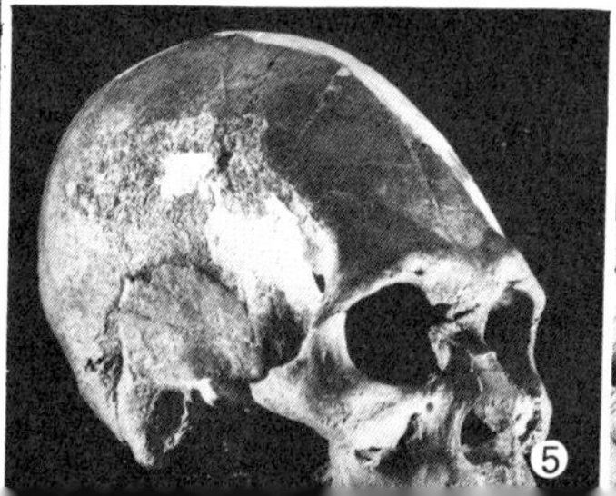

2 - Watercraft were used by Aboriginals to reach Australia. 3 - Skeleton of 3,000 year old dingo excavated at Fromm's Landing, S.A. 4 - The famous Talgai skull found in Q/ld. 5 - Fossilised skull from the Kow Swamp burial site, Vic. 6 - Excavations at Kintore Cave, N.T., provide evidence of man's life in Australia.

Tribal Lands

In 1788 when European settlement began in Australia an estimated 250,000 to 300,000 Aboriginals were living in distinct groups throughout the continent. Numbers declined dramatically with the colonization of Australia, sometimes without direct contact with the white man. Whole groups vanished within a few years due to introduced diseases and conflicts. Small-pox which reached plague proportions among the Aboriginals of the Sydney District in 1798, spread from group to group down the river systems, reaching distant Adelaide and decimating the population long before the exploration or settlement of that part of the continent.

In recent years there has been a sharp increase in the population of the remaining groups in remote areas. Today there are some 45,000 Aboriginals of unmixed descent. A total of over 106,000 people identified themselves as of Aboriginal descent at the 1971 census and it is estimated that the population will reach 300,000 before the end of the century.

Daily life was carried on in small groups of closely related men and their families called bands. In many areas these bands, numbering from 20 to 50 individuals, were loosely associated with other bands to form groups, sometimes called tribes.

An estimated 500 to 600 tribal associations of 100 to 1,000 people at one time existed in Australia. Each of these occupied a defined territory demarcated by natural barriers such as rivers, mountain ranges or deserts.

The size of the area used by a local band depended mainly upon the capacity of the land to produce natural plant and animal foods. Central Australian groups ranged over large tracts of territory while in the sub-tropical north, in the fertile river valleys (such as the Murray-Darling basin) and along the coasts, larger numbers were supported on comparatively small areas.

There were probably about 300 distinct Australian languages. Many of these included several dialects, in all numbering some 600. Aboriginal languages have some basic similarities in vocabulary and sound system but can differ significantly in their grammatical structure. They are marked by precision and brevity of expression. Besides the everyday spoken word the Aboriginals in some areas had special languages for use in sacred rituals, songs, and for use when talking to particular close relatives.

Many languages are still spoken, the most widely used being the several dialects of the Western Desert language. One of these, Pitjantjatjara, is taught regularly each year in Adelaide and Alice Springs.

1 - Ayers Rock, important mythological centre, C.A. 2 - Stone quarry, central desert, Yuendumu, C.A. 3 - Arnhem Land, escarpment. 4 - The Olgas, C.A. 5 - Flinders Ranges, home of the "Hills" people. 6 - The Murray Valley had the densest population in prehistoric Australia. 7 - Water being brought into camp. 8 - Billabongs, a rich source of food. 9 - The Bluff, S.A. features in local legends. 10 - Pandanus palms provided materials for baskets and mats.

The Men's Way of Life

The contrasting conditions under which the Aboriginals lived influenced to a large extent the time available for different pursuits. Food gathering was of paramount importance and in the central deserts a considerable amount of time was devoted to hunting. On the coast and in the rich river valleys, food supplies were more regular, allowing greater preoccupation with other activities.

The men were essentially hunters and fishermen supplying meat to supplement the staple vegetable foods gathered by the women and children. Kangaroos, emus, possums, large goannas and snakes were speared, clubbed or captured in pit-falls, nets, traps or noose snares. Wombats and other burrowing animals were smoked or dug out of their burrows. Clubs and boomerangs were thrown among flocks of birds, sometimes to drive them into hidden nets. Fish were speared or caught with traps, hooks, handnets, or by poisoning pools with plant juices. In the north, turtles, dugong, dolphins, crocodiles and large fish were harpooned and flying foxes beaten down from trees with sticks. Seals were an important source of food on the southern coasts and Tasmania.

The skills of tracking and hunting were taught from childhood. The foot tracks of every member of the group could be identified on sight. The Aboriginal has extraordinary ability to follow his prey by reading signs such as broken twigs, displaced stones or faint markings on the ground.

The men were the tool makers, devoting much time to the skilful conversion of stone, wood, bark, bone and fibre into a wide range of weapons, utensils and ceremonial objects. Throughout Australia many different tools and weapons were made but generally a small basic set was used to ensure ease and freedom of movement while hunting and food-gathering. Many, such as the long, concave, central Australian spear-thrower, had a multiple function: used primarily to project a spear, these could also serve as dishes for food or ceremonial decorations; a stone chisel mounted on the end turned the spear-thrower into a wood-working tool; it was sometimes used to dig or clear the ground; when fire was needed the edge of the hard-wood spear-thrower was rubbed vigorously on a piece of soft-wood to produce smouldering wood powder.

Ceremonial ritual dominated the life of the men. Introduction to beliefs, songs and ritual began at an early age and instruction continued throughout a man's life. Understanding of tribal law and custom deepened after youths completed the first stages of initiation usually as boys of twelve to fourteen years. Special authority was vested in those mature men who had the deepest understanding of tribal law and customs and were strong in character. These individuals were leaders in ceremonial matters and in decision-making generally.

1 - Men's camp, Musgrave Ranges, S.A. 2 - Welcoming dance, Aranda Tribe, Alice Springs. 3 - Decorating burial pole, Melville Island. 4 - Arnhem Land barramundi, part of the basic diet. 5 - Returning from the hunt. 6 - Killing snake, Arnhem Land. 7 - The dog was the Aboriginals' only domesticated animal. 8 - Decorating beanwood shields, C.A. 9 - Shaping a spear-thrower.

The Women's Way of Life

Women were the main food collectors, providing a larger proportion of a group's daily needs than the men. Long hours were devoted to gathering plant foods and smaller animals from desert, forest, swamp and sea shore. The skill of the Aboriginals in locating food supplies, even in the driest deserts, ensured a constant diet of nutritious foods, except in the poorest of seasons.

Tortoises, snakes, shell-fish, crabs and other marine life were caught in lagoons, marshes and on coastal reefs. Inland, lizards, snakes, witchetty grubs, honey ants and small marsupials were obtained by digging with a sharpened stick. Fruit, flowers, manna and honey were a vital source of sugar. Roots, yams, grass seeds for 'bread'; nothing was overlooked in the quest for food. Seasonal delicacies such as eggs of the turtle and water birds provided a welcome change of diet.

The preparation and cooking of food was usually a task for women. Seeds were gathered, winnowed in bark or wooden dishes, and then ground between stones with water to make a paste which was either eaten raw or moulded into flat, oval 'cakes' and cooked in hot ashes.

The typical earth oven was formed by lighting a fire in a shallow depression in the ground. Once the fire had died down the animal would be placed in the hole and covered with hot ashes and earth. Sometimes a bed of leaves was placed on the hot coals beneath the animal or vegetable and a covering of leaves added before the oven was sealed with earth. Heated stones or pieces of ant bed were often placed on the coals to retain more heat. Occasionally water would be poured into the oven through a hole made in the top of the mound to generate steam. Animals were cooked in their skins.

The main meal was usually in the evening when most of the product of the day's hunting and gathering was cooked. Remnants of the evening meal served for the following morning.

During the day the women ate fruit and berries and sampled other plant and animal foods. All enjoyed witchetty grubs obtained by digging out the roots of infested shrubs or by chopping them out from branches of gum trees. These larvae are rich in calories, protein and fat and ten large grubs are sufficient to provide the daily needs of an adult.

The women were responsible for fetching drinking water and firewood, they cared for the babies and helped in building the family hut or shade. Their crafts included the manufacture of string bags, baskets, nets, mats and ornaments.

The women participated in secular ceremonies and certain phases of sacred ones and in some areas had a secret ritual life of their own.

1 - Grinding grass seeds. 2 - Winnowing grass seeds. 3 - Cleaning **small** bulbs. 4 - Women bring wood into camp. 5, 6 - Witchetty grubs are a nutritious item of diet, C.A. 7 - Women digging yams. 8 - Wooden carrying dish balances delicately on head. 9 - Hand fishing with scoop nets.

Dwellings

Each family made its own sleeping area and associated fire place. In relatively permanent camps and in rainy times, they would build shelters or huts. The position of huts in a camp reflected the relationships of the families occupying them. Even movement within a camp was controlled by a code of behaviour. Fathers, mothers and their young children slept as a family unit. Uninitiated youths and single men kept to a separate part of the camp and often there was a hut set aside for widows and single women.

Temporary wind-breaks and simple shades were used over a wide area at most times of the year. More permanent shelters were normally round or rectangular in shape, although there were marked regional differences in style, construction techniques and raw materials.

In central Australia the weather-proof shelter or *wiltja* was constructed with arched boughs set firmly into the ground in an oval or circle and secured at the apex. Spinifex, brush or leafy boughs were used to cover the framework.

Although simple in design the *wiltja* was ideally suited to the environment of the central deserts and demonstrates the skill of the Aboriginals in converting limited resources into efficient dwellings. The rounded shape presented least resistance to wind while the outer covering acted as both insulation and filter to ensure that only clean air entered the hut. The dark interior discouraged the prolific number of flies so common to the Australian outback. A constant fire burning near the entrance or at times in the hut, provided needed warmth during the cold and frosty nights.

More elaborate shelters were needed in the tropical north where heavy rains are a feature of the summer wet season. These were formed from a framework of saplings covered by overlapping sheets of bark. Sometimes huts were built on stilts to enable a smouldering fire to be maintained beneath the floor to discourage mosquitos. In coastal regions seaweed was sometimes used to cover a bough framework and mud was smeared over the exterior to provide further protection against wind and rain.

Where available, rock shelters and shallow caves were often occupied during wet weather. These cave shelters were sometimes painted elaborately for sorcery purposes or hunting or love magic. Camp debris discarded on cave floors built up gradually over many thousands of years to provide a record of the life of the occupants. Careful excavation and examination of these deposits by the archaeologist enables the local environment to be reconstructed in great detail. Cave deposits date back more than 20,000 years in Australia.

When game and edible fruits were exhausted, and water supplies became inadequate, the camp was moved to a new site. A camp would be abandoned also when a person died. Often smoky fires were lit to conceal the departure of relatives from the spirits of the deceased.

1 - Community Bark Shelter, Arnhem Land. 2 - Men's camp, C.A. 3 - Paperbark bed in rock shelter. 4 - Stringybark hut on stilts. 5 - Bark is used while fresh and pliable. 6 - Solid hut framework, Coopers Creek. 7 - Camp with grass covered wurleys. 8 - Rock shelters protect in wet weather.

Fire Making

Fire was essential to the Australian Aboriginal for warmth, cooking, illumination and a range of specialized purposes.

Usually fire was made by friction created with a fire-drill or fire-saw. To use a fire-drill, a pit was made in a soft-wood stick, or sometimes a shield. A thin hard-wood 'drill' was rapidly twirled between the palms of the hands as they were moved up and down the drill-stick. This action produced smouldering wood powder which was tipped on to tinder, blown gently and swung in the air. Ignition took about a minute.

The other friction method of making fire was by means of a 'fire-saw'. The edge of a hard-wood stick would be drawn rapidly to and fro across a cleft stick containing tinder. In central Australia a hard-wood spear-thrower was rubbed across a soft-wood shield to produce the smouldering wood powder.

Fire was obtained occasionally by striking a piece of flint held on a pad of tinder with a piece of ironstone or iron pyrites. The sparks dropped on to tinder and ignited.

Dried grass, finely shredded bark, dead leaves, bird feathers, animal hair and fur, were used as tinder in all methods of fire making.

The Aboriginals made fire to a pre-judged level of heat. Hard-woods were selected to generate hot coals for efficient cooking; a low flame could be produced when heat was required to soften gum which was obtained from the spinifex or other plants and used to mount stone tools on handles or the ends of spear-throwers. These gums are thermo-plastics, softening upon heating to a low temperature and becoming extremely hard when cold. Dried leaves and light brush were used to provide brilliant illumination during night ceremonies.

Fire was used often as an aid on hunting expeditions. Spinifex and other grasses, fired in the right quarter, could result in a harvest of game as animals escaping from the flames were speared or clubbed.

To preserve a vital source of warmth in wet weather a fire was kept alight at all times. A fire-stick would be carried carefully from camp to camp and sometimes deposited in a cave, hollow log or other sheltered place. A smouldering fire-stick could be quickly brought back to life by swinging it vigorously through the air.

1 - Fire drill, Kimberleys, W.A. 2 - Fire is kept burning at all times. 3 - A burning branch provides heat when away from camp. 4 - Earth oven, Arnhem Land. 5 - Earth ovens were used throughout the continent. 6, 7, 8, 9 - Friction creates smouldering wood powder which is placed on dry grass and ignites in the wind.

Religion and Ceremonies

Aboriginal ceremonial life expressed religious and spiritual values through the continuation of the traditions of the mythological past. It was believed to have an economic function also by ensuring the supply of vegetable foods, game and water.

Religious systems in which men are identified with animals, plants and natural phenomena and where these are used to distinguish groupings in society, are called 'totemism'. In Aboriginal belief these 'totems' could be influenced and manipulated by ceremonies conducted by their human 'kinsmen'.

Members of groups with totemic affiliation in the central and southern regions of Australia performed increase ceremonies at ritual centres to maintain the natural species and to ensure the survival of the tribal group. Open only to fully initiated men, increase rituals were a most sacred and secret part of ritual life. In northern Australia emphasis was on mortuary rites and the afterlife.

The spirit ancestors of the mythological past included the Fertility Mother and other ancestral women of Arnhem Land, great snake ancestors in the Kimberleys and Northern Territory, bands of human and animal totemic spirits in central Australia, and sky-heroes in eastern Australia. Their lives and activities as creators of the physical world, of its human inhabitants, of the animal and plant life, and of tribal customs, were re-enacted in age-old ceremonies.

Youths were initiated into the sacred beliefs and secret rites and into a code of discipline and behaviour maintained by the older men. The initiates went through fire ordeals and ritual operations such as tooth evulsion, circumcision and sub-incision. These practices are still carried out in some parts of central and northern Australia.

Sacred objects known in central Australia as *tjuringa* were made from pieces of wood or stone. Circular or elongate they were smoothed and engraved with stylised designs, usually on both sides. The patterns provided a cue for the legendary stories told during ceremonial ritual. Such objects could not be seen by women and children, on pain of death.

The sacred bullroarers, long flat wooden objects like the wooden *tjuringa*, with symbolic designs incised on both surfaces, were used by many tribes to warn the uninitiated of a secret ritual. Bullroarers were whirled over the head on a piece of hair-string, making a distinctive sound which was recognized by all as a sign that a ceremony was in progress.

In many regions elaborate ground drawings were an integral part of ceremonial ritual. The *bora* or initiation grounds of New South Wales are well known for their large and elaborate designs including recumbent figures moulded in earth or clay. Massive geometric motifs carved on the trunks of gum trees are usually associated with these sites.

1 - Pukamuni ceremony, Melville Is. 1911. 2 - *Pulapa* ceremony, Ernabella, S.A. 3 - Pukamuni burial rituals. 4 - Elaborate 'bora' gound, N.S.W. 5 - Carved ceremonial tree, N.S.W. 6 - Body painting was often elaborate. 7 - Sand drawings, C.A. 8 - Ceremonial ritual, Adelaide 1845.

Magic and Medicine

Supernatural forces were blamed for almost every mishap or disaster known to the Aboriginals. The only corrective measures possible were through magic and ritual.

Medicine-men were greatly respected and cured illness sometimes by supposedly extracting a piece of quartz, bone or evil blood from the painful part of the body, which they massaged and sucked. In some areas a wound was covered with a clay poultice and smeared with blood, fat or perspiration. Charms were believed to ward off illness but plants with medicinal properties were known and widely used.

Sorcerers were universally feared as they could cause the death or blindness of a victim by projecting an evil spirit or object into him with a 'pointing-bone', or by capturing his spirit in a piece of his hair or food.

Central Australian sorcerers wore *kurdaitja* shoes, made of emu feathers and human blood, to conceal their footprints. Quartz and other crystals symbolising magical powers were used in causing death or illness, to bring rain, and to bring about success in love. Pebbles, pearl-shells, australites (tektites) and many kinds of ornaments served as media of magic, and as charms of various kinds.

In the lower Murray Valley bones or the remains of animals which had been eaten were used as a medium of sorcery. A particular bone of a bird or animal eaten by an enemy was mixed with grease, red ochre and human hair. The resulting mass was stuck in a lump on the end of a prepared skewer of kangaroo's leg bone and when injury was to be inflicted on the person who had eaten the animal, the object was placed near the fire. As the knob melted, so disease was supposed to be engendered in the person being bewitched, and if it wholly melted he died.

'Bone pointing' was practised by many groups. Short pieces of bone, pointed at one end and often tipped at the other with a small lump of gum to which was attached a length of human hair string, were used to deadly effect. Some 'pointing bones' (shaped sticks were also used) were decorated with fine cuts or covered with bird down. Among the Aranda people of central Australia a man wishing to use a 'pointing bone' first went away into the bush, placed the bone in the ground and repeated curses over it. Later, in the darkness of night it would be pointed secretly at the victim with repeated magical formulae and chants. The boned person would sicken and eventually die unless some medicine man could discover and remove the evil magic.

Special rites were carried out to bring rain to freshen the countryside, to reveal the tracks of game in the wet soil, to hide the tracks of a criminal, and to augment the water supply. Both men and women carried out magical rites to ensure success in love, as did hunters who sought to stupify game and make it easy to kill.

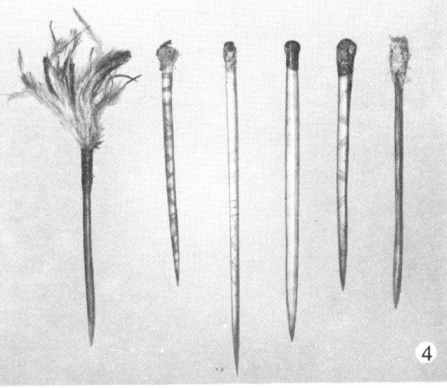
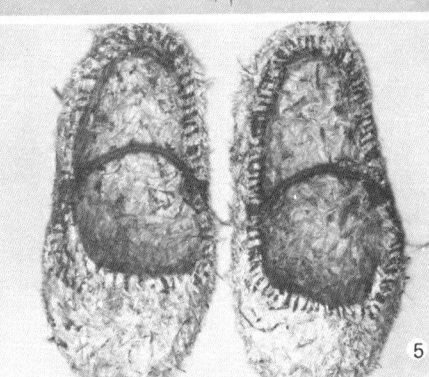

1 - Medicine man, Aranda Tribe, C.A. 2 - Bone pointing, Dieri Tribe, S.A. 3 - Bone pointing, Aranda Tribe, C.A. 4 - Pointing bones. 5 - The Aranda of Central Australia believed that a death was invariably due to evil magical influences of some enemy. When the guilt, rightly or wrongly, was fixed upon a particular person, either a man called 'kurdaitja' was chosen to avenge the death, or an individual would go forth on his own initiative. To cover his tracks he wore the shoes to which white men attached the name 'kurdaitja', though it properly belongs to the man himself. 6 - Medicine man sucking and massaging patient to withdraw evil spirit.

Games and Music

Children were treated with great affection. Their play was largely imitative of adult economic and social life.

Boys practised with toy weapons and at identifying tracks. Small discs of bark were cut from gum trees and bowled along the ground as targets for miniature spears. In regions where boomerangs were used small models were made and thrown with great skill. Play and schooling for future life were inseparable in the Aboriginal world.

Girls played camp games and accompanied their mothers on food collecting expeditions. Each young girl went armed with a small digging stick of her own to dig out lizards and witchetty grubs.

All children learnt songs, dancing, mythological tales, sand drawing and string games; they would run, swim, wrestle, fight, slide on mud into creeks, roll in the sand and climb trees.

The Lake Eyre tribes of South Australia made small round balls from burnt gypsum mixed with water which were spun on a hard surface. The person whose ball spun for the longest time was the winner. A somewhat larger ball, with a small peg fixed in the centre, was used by the women for the same game. Still larger and more solid balls were bowled from opposite sides of a clay pan by two teams of men. The object being to break up the opponents' balls while they were in motion.

Another game played by the men involved throwing a wooden play-stick or *wit-wit* so that it ricochetted off the hard ground. Many games were contested by opposing sides drawn from different social groups within the tribe.

Music was an important part of Aboriginal cultural life, and every man memorized many hundreds of verses of songs. Dances — mostly imitative of animals and human or spiritual beings were performed to the accompaniment of songs or chants. A stick or stone beaten on the ground, the clapping of hands one against the other or on the thighs, or pairs of clap-sticks or boomerangs tapped together set the time for dancers and singers. In some areas women used rolls of skin or small bags for this purpose.

In the north of the Northern Territory the *didjeridu* or drone pipe made from a portion of a small tree trunk hollowed out by termites or a section of bamboo, up to three metres long, provided a rhythm accompaniment.

For some of the rituals of Arnhem Land, solid and hollow logs, up to two metres in length, were used as drums, being struck at regular intervals throughout the ceremony. These were sacred instruments, often painted with elaborate designs.

1 - Tree climbing in search of wood grubs, possums and honey. 2 - Practising with shield and boomerang. 3 - Digging edible roots, Musgrave Ranges, S.A. 4 - The Didjeridu is a wind instrument made from a tree trunk. 5 - Young Aboriginal dancers. 6 - Football has become a popular sport. 7 - Children love the water, Maningrida, N.T. 8 - Father teaches son to dig rabbits. 9 - Children learn about cultural life from infancy. 10 - *Numidi* digs for honey ants.

Dress and Ornament

Little or no clothing was worn in most areas. In the hot centre and north of Australia everyday 'dress' might consist of hair string armlets, necklets, and forehead-bands, a bone nose-pin and a hair string or fur apron or tassel hanging in front from a waist string.

Bark waist-belts were worn in many parts of northern Australia; during mourning ceremonies on Melville and Bathurst Islands the women wore elaborately decorated bark armlets painted with traditional designs. The most striking armlets were decorated with colourful birds' feathers.

Cloaks and rugs made from animal skins were worn frequently in the colder south. The most favoured skin for this purpose was the dense, warm, but light skin of the possum. The fur was usually worn next to the body and decorative patterns cut on the outer surface with a mussel shell or stone flake. Along the Coorong of South Australia an unusual variation was a cloak woven from strands of sea-weed.

A wide range of pendants and necklaces was worn in all parts of Australia, these being made from seeds, seed pods, claws, shells, animal tails, small jaw bones and sections of grass. In central Australia chaplets of animal bones were worn by widows. Necklaces of kangaroo incisor teeth, either set in gum or beeswax, or bound together with sinews, were popular, The binding was painted with red ochre to make the teeth stand out against the dark body of the Aboriginal.

The most remarkable necklace to be found in Australia came from a single 7000 years old grave at Lake Nitchie in the River Darling region of New South Wales. It was made from one hundred and eighty pierced teeth of the Tasmanian Devil, *Sarcophilus harrissii*, extinct on the Australian mainland for thousands of years. The root ends of the teeth have been ground down carefully to enable easy piercing. This ancient necklace is the only example of its kind found in Australia and resembles similar specimens from the Paleolithic sites in Europe.

On ceremonial occasions decorations were colourful and elaborate. Special ornaments of many types were worn, often forming a composite pattern with painted body designs. Feather down and finely chopped grass coloured with ochres were stuck on the body with human blood to form striking decorative patterns. These decorations took many hours to prepare, as the intricate designs had to conform to an established code which demanded perfection.

Ornamental scars or cicatrices were cut on the body with a shell or stone knife and the wound filled with ashes so that it healed into a raised scar. Patterns of cicatrices proudly worn by both men and women sometimes covered the body from the shoulders to the knees. These generally served purely for decoration, and might be made at initiation, marriage or other stages of life.

1 - Dressed for the Pukamuni, Bathurst Is., N.T. 2 - Kangaroo tooth ornament, N.T. 3 - Gum leaves as a body decoration. 4, 5 - Skin cloaks were widely used in the south. 6 - Teeth from the remarkable Lake Nitchie necklace. 7 - Mourning armlets, Melville Is., N.T. 8 - Rare tooth necklace excavated at Roonka, S.A. 9 - Warramunga woman, N.T. 10 - Body scarring was widely practised.

Watercraft

When Europeans arrived in Australia watercraft, in the form of wood, reed and bark rafts, and bark and log canoes, were in use in nearly all the better watered parts of the continent. On the lakes of the lower Murray River the women used rafts constructed from layers of reeds to reach mussel beds far from the shore. Eight to ten women would occupy one raft which was propelled with a long pole. The women dived from the rafts in search of shellfish and crayfish. On the raft food was cooked over a fire built on a platform of wet sea-weed and sand.

Explorers also noted a number of distinct types of canoes. The simplest craft was made from a large sheet of thick bark. The ends were pointed and the bark manipulated while fresh and pliable to form a crude boat which was used for crossing rivers and lagoons, and for fishing. They were usually propelled by punting with a long pole. The fragile nature of these simple craft limited their use to the protected inland waters of the Murray-Darling basin, western Victoria and the south-east of South Australia.

On the rivers and creeks of coastal New South Wales and in south-east Victoria a second type of canoe was used. These were made from large cylindrical sheets of bark which were turned inside-out and bound at the ends with fibre rope. The outer bark shell of the canoe was straightened by rod-shaped stretchers fixed across the canoe and pliant branches forced into the body to act as ribs.

More sophisticated craft were in use on the tropical northern and Queensland coasts. Of two basic types (the sewn bark canoe and the dug-out canoe), they were superior to those of the southern water-ways, and allowed men to venture out to sea for long periods.

The sewn canoe was constructed from broad strips of bark stitched together and strengthened with a network of ties, stretchers, braces and ribs. Poles were lashed along the bulwarks to act as gunwales and to prevent the sides from collapsing.

Dugout canoes in northern Australia were made in imitation of similar craft brought by the Macassan trepang fleets from Indonesia during the last few centuries.

1 - Canoe scar on river gum, Blanchetown, S.A. 2, 3 - Soft-wood rafts, northwest W.A. 4 - Macassan praus featured in Groote Eylandt cave art. 5 - Canoes extended the hunt. 6 - Bark canoes were common in the Murray Valley. 7 - Sewing bark canoe with cane and wallaby bone point, Q/ld. 8 - Murray River bark canoe under construction, 1862. 9 - Aboriginals adapt quickly to introduced tools, N.T.

Hunting and Fighting

A strict system of punishment upheld the social and religious structure of Aboriginal society. Feuding occurred mainly between clans or local groups, but camp fights were a common event. Vendettas were carried on for years between clans and could result in many deaths. The main purpose of warfare was to avenge an insult or crime or to capture women, but not to take the land or other possessions of an enemy. The most serious crimes were murder, the stealing of women, incest, and ritual offences.

After a wrong had been committed a revenge party would surround a camp at night, or walk in at daylight and kill a man to avenge the death of a member of their clan or local group. In pitched battles up to fifteen men could be killed but combats usually stopped when one or two were fatally injured.

Spears, boomerangs and clubs were the main offensive weapons. Of these, spears were the most frequently used and a formidable weapon in the hands of an Aboriginal trained in their use since childhood. They were also used to hunt and fish; some served as sacred objects.

A wide range of spears was made with distinctive characteristics. They varied in length from a little over one metre to nearly four metres and often had tips of pointed or barbed hard-wood, bone, stone or stingray spines. Cultural contact provided metal, wire and glass to replace traditional materials. In order to cause infection spear-heads were dipped in a putrid body, smeared with grass-tree gum or the milky juice of the mangrove. Some spears were used in the hand but most were thrown with a spear-thrower which varied in shape and size according to the type of spear used. These objects simply extended the length of the arm to provide added leverage for the launch.

Finely balanced heavy wooden clubs could be wielded with deadly effect. A distinctive type, often made from the wood of the sheoak tree, was the boomerang-shaped club of south-eastern Australia.

Shields were employed as defence against spear and club. Made of bark, soft or hard-wood, they varied in size, shape and decoration from region to region. Hard-wood parrying shields, with their finely incised geometric patterns, were used mainly in south-eastern Australia, while broader shields were common in other areas.

In north-eastern Queensland large slabs cut from the root-flanges of giant fig trees and fashioned into shields, completely protected a combatant from blows aimed with a large hard-wood fighting sword.

1 - Launching a spear, S.A. 2 - A duel with clubs, C.A. 3 - Fighting shield (with abstract scorpion design) and sword, Q/ld. 4 - Kangaroo hunters, C.A. 5 - Aboriginal fish traps, Darling River. 6 - Aboriginals are highly skilled with the spear. 7 - Cutting wood for spear-thrower, C.A. 8 - Returning home from the hunt.

The Boomerang

The boomerang has become a symbol of the Australian Aboriginals although similar weapons, used as throwing sticks, were known in ancient Egypt and parts of South America.

Australian boomerangs developed from throwing sticks and clubs and most were hurled at an enemy or prey. They were made or were traded for use over a very wide area but did not occur in some parts of the continent, including Arnhem Land, Cape York, Tasmania and the other offshore islands.

Boomerangs came in many sizes and shapes. The most interesting type was the returning boomerang. An Australian invention, its use was limited to games, killing birds and directing animals into traps. Light and thin, with a deep curvature in relation to length, the ends are slightly twisted in opposite directions while the lower surface is flat and the upper surface convex. They were used in most areas where the boomerang existed, except in central and northern Australia.

The most widely used non-returning boomerang was the central Australian type. Made from a carefully selected curved limb of a mulga tree it has fluting on the upper surface and a flat under side neatly finished with adze marks. These boomerangs were given a coating of red ochre. When used in ceremonies they were often painted with decorative white, yellow and black designs.

A special fighting boomerang was made in central Australia with a distinctive 'hook' on one end to catch on a shield and swing the weapon around to strike the defender.

The largest boomerangs, measuring up to two metres in length, were used in western Queensland and along Cooper Creek to the Lake Eyre region of South Australia. Some were rounded on both sides and beautifully finished with fine grooves or fluting; others had intricate incised geometric patterns on the upper surface.

In common with other Aboriginal weapons the boomerang had a multiplicity of uses. Besides its normal function as a fighting or hunting weapon it served to clear grass and soil to prepare comfortable camp-sites or ceremonial grounds; it was used as a poker and shovel when cooking, the ashes being scraped away to make room for a carcase and the cooked food also being raked out from the ashes. The sharp end of a hard-wood boomerang was sometimes employed for cutting up a cooked animal or for digging holes for an earth oven or the erection of ceremonial regalia; outcrops of stone were dug out with boomerangs to obtain unweathered material for implements; the sharp edge could be used to create friction in fire-making; two of these weapons tapped together were sometimes an accompaniment to ceremonies, the rapid vibrating sound only being properly made by experts. Other boomerangs served as sacred objects.

1 - Boomerangs were many shapes. 2 - Fighting with boomerangs, Dieri Tribe, S.A. 3 - C.A. boomerangs were made of mulga-wood. 4 - Men with fighting weapons. 5 - Hunter waiting for game. 6 - Smoothing a boomerang, Dieri Tribe. 7 - Sharpening stone tools with boomerang. 8 - Trimming digging stick.

Material Possessions

The hunter-gatherer existence led by the Aboriginals limited the number and size of objects that could be transported from one camp to another. However, full use was made of natural resources to produce a range of items for everyday use. Throughout the different groups a high degree of craftsmanship was exhibited, but local conditions and requirements resulted in marked variations in the objects produced.

A wide range of string and cord was spun by both men and women from human hair, animal fur, bark and root fibres, reeds and leaves of palm trees. The fibres were plied out on the thigh with one hand while spinning them on to a simple wooden bobbin with the other. The string and cord were made into nets, baskets, mats and fishing lines. In some parts of Arnhem Land baskets were made from sheets of bark and decorated with patterns in red, yellow, white and black ochres.

Wooden dishes were widely used to carry babies, water, food and small household articles while some types served as spades for digging. They were made from both the softwood of Sturt's bean tree, *Erythrina vespertilio*, and the eucalypt, *Eucalyptus rostrata*. The shape of the vessels varied from shallow to steep-sided. In central Australia, where dishes were in everyday use, the surface was finished with fine fluting or adze marks. In an emergency a temporary dish could be obtained by cutting an oval piece of bark from a gum tree. Women became very skilled at balancing loaded dishes on their heads with the aid of grass or hair ring pads.

Bailer and other large shells were used in coastal areas as water and food carriers.

Some groups prepared serviceable and strong water bags from animal skins. After killing, the animal was opened around the neck and the skin rolled back and peeled from the body. The leg and tail apertures were tied with cord, the fur singed off and the whole skin soaked for several hours in an astringent fluid made from acacia bark. These useful carriers could hold up to twenty-five litres of precious water.

Plant and tree gums, essential to seal containers, repair weapons and attach stone tools to handles, were extracted from spinifex grass, the bloodwood, acacia, and numerous other species. In northern Australia bees-wax was in common use.

Large simple flakes of stone provided with gum handles were used effectively as knives. When not in use, sheaths of soft bark protected the sharp edges from damage.

1 - Water-carriers were in universal use in C.A. 2 - Baskets from the East Alligator River, Arnhem Land. 3 - Bark baskets were decorated with abstract designs. 4 - Mounted adze used to form wooden utensils, Dieri Tribe, S.A. 5 - Weaving with stick, Archer River, Q/ld. 6 - Circular threaded mat used as shade or ground-cover. 7 - Weaving basket, Archer River, Q/ld. 8 - Spinning animal fur. 9 - Skin water-carrier.

Stone Tools

The Aboriginals made wide use of different types of stone to produce a range of tools for shaping wooden weapons and domestic utensils, to cut meat, scar the body and open veins to obtain blood, chop grass into fine pieces for use in ceremonial decoration, prepare skins for use as cloaks and countless other functions.

In his practical approach to daily problems the Aboriginal used available materials to great advantage. Small rounded pebbles served as hammers to flake implements, grind ochre and crush bones to obtain marrow. Large sized pebbles and flat slabs of stone were used as pounders and grinders to reduce seeds to a usable flour or paste.

Fine-grained stones such as flint, jasper, agate, chert and porcellanite were highly prized and traded widely in different parts of the continent. Quartzite, quartz and sandstone were used when more suitable material was in short supply. In some areas australites (tektites) were fashioned into small, sharp implements. Tough diorites and basaltic rocks were made into edge-ground axes.

There are many well-known and extensive sites where stone was quarried regularly over many thousands of years. At these sites discarded flakes sometimes form mounds many metres thick and provide important evidence of the techniques used in tool making.

The earliest tools were formed from large pieces of stone, pebbles or flakes. One margin was usually sharpened to a working edge by striking off small flakes with a rounded, water-worn pebble. These tools relied upon weight and force to cut wood and shape it into artifacts.

Several thousand years ago the Aboriginals developed the technique of flake knapping. This involved roughly shaping a piece of stone (a core) by the removal of a number of primary flakes to enable smaller pieces of a pre-determined shape to be struck off. This led to the manufacture of a number of new forms including leaf-shaped points such as the well-known uniface *pirri* and the bi-face 'Kimberley' point. The *pirri* was in use in the Murray Valley 4,000 years ago. Smaller tool types had to be mounted in gum on handles to enable sufficient force to be applied for effective use.

At the time of European settlement one of the most widely used tools was the adze or *tula*. Mounted in gum on a slightly curved wooden handle or the butt of a spear-thrower, this semi-discoidal implement, with its carefully trimmed cutting edge, was a multi-purpose tool employed for adzing, chopping and scraping. Such tools were re-sharpened by striking with a small hammerstone, the flat of a boomerang, or forcing small flakes off with the teeth. Reduced or worn-out forms are found in great numbers on many old camp-sites.

Stone objects are the most durable evidence of long-past occupation by Aboriginal groups. Collection and study of different types concentrated on eroded surface camp-sites and in undisturbed rock shelter deposits, provide evidence of the culture of the Aboriginals over the past 30,000 years.

1 - Flint pebble supply, lower south-east S.A. 2 - Stone flake used to smooth handle of mounted adze, C.A. 3 - Beating spinifex grass to obtain globules of gum. 4 - Fusing gum with hot stone. 5 - Striking flake from core. 6 - Edge-grinding an axehead. 7 - Drawing tendon from kangaroo tail. 8 - Cutting bark dish with natural stone.

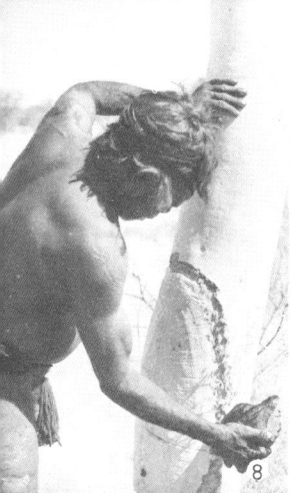

Bone Artifacts

Bones sharpened to a fine point were employed as spear tips, fish gouges, harpoon heads, pegs for spear-throwers, as tools for shaping or pressure-flaking specialized stone implements and as death pointers or murder weapons.

Fine awls and needles, made from a leg bone of an emu or kangaroo, were pointed by careful rubbing on the surface of a stone and then used to pierce skins which were sewn together to serve as cloaks or rugs.

In Arnhem Land human-bone bark strippers were used and the shoulder blades of kangaroos made into yam-slicers. Emu leg-bone gouges are known from Cape York.

Animal jaws and teeth had wide use as scrapers, borers and incisors. The lower jaws of the kangaroo and wallaby were frequently used, while dingo incisors served to gouge the intricate totemic designs on the surface of sacred objects.

It was the custom of men and women of many groups to wear a bone through the septum of the nose as a form of personal adornment. In the case of boys, aged ten to twelve or even younger, the septum was pierced by a close relative. A sharpened leg bone of the kangaroo was used for the operation and the hole kept open during healing with the aid of a short piece of bamboo or stick. The same operation was performed on young girls by the husband immediately after marriage.

In parts of Victoria a noose made from cord formed of strands of twine made from the roots of the bulrush was used to strangle human victims. A sharpened point about fifteen centimetres long, made from the leg bone of a kangaroo was attached to one end. The bone was slid under the victim's neck, put through a loop at the other end of the cord and quickly drawn tight.

Perhaps the most unusual use of bone was in the lakes area of the lower Murray and along the Coorong where the local Aboriginals used human skulls as water carriers. Skulls of deceased parents and close relatives were preferred to those of strangers.

Bone artifacts had a continent-wide distribution and have survived in both occupation and burial sites. Large concentrations are recorded from excavated sites in South Australia, Victoria, New South Wales and Tasmania. Similar implements found in the Fromm's Landing excavation on the Murray River in South Australia extended to a depth of nearly five metres and have been dated to about 5,000 years ago.

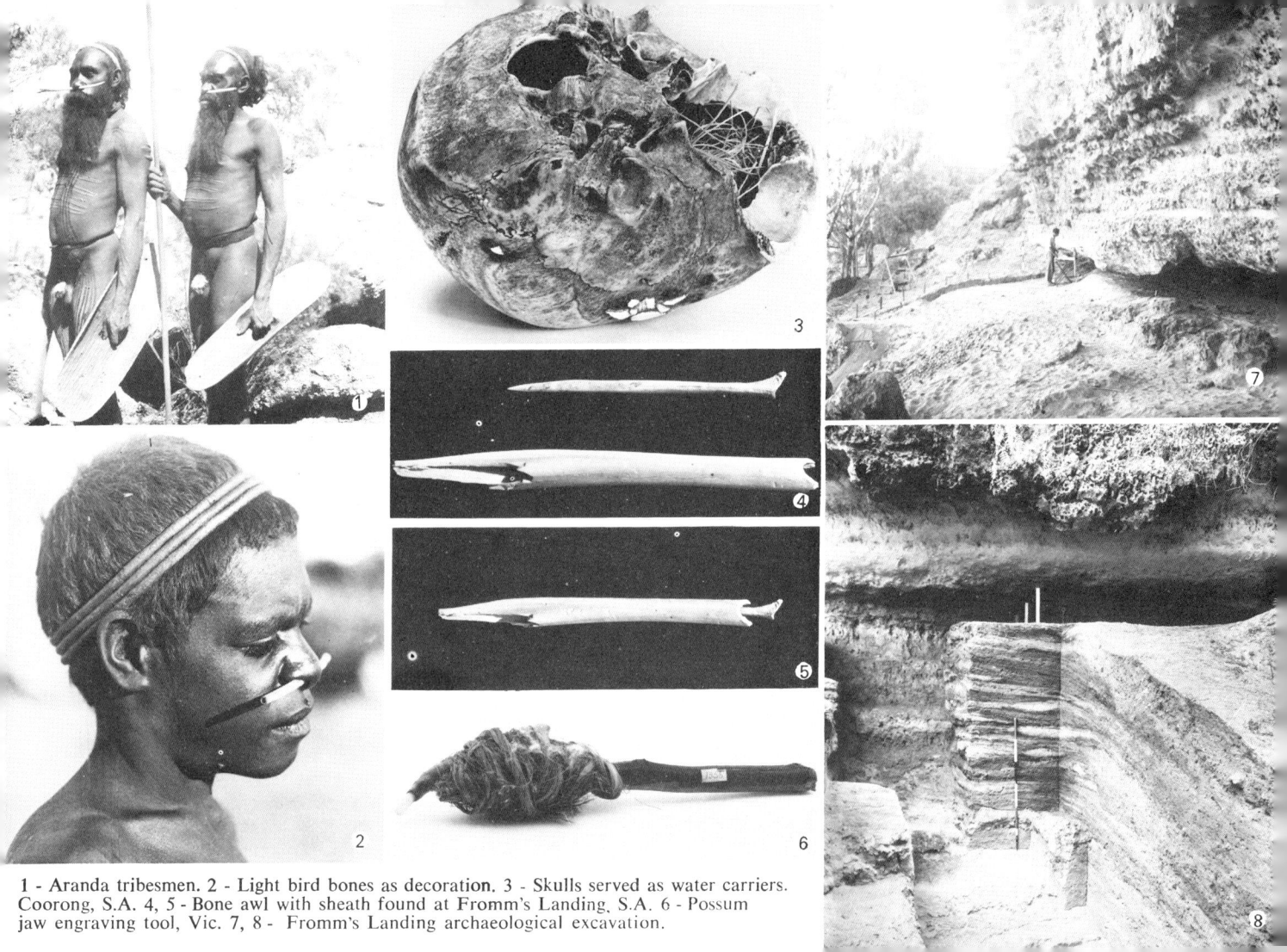

1 - Aranda tribesmen. 2 - Light bird bones as decoration. 3 - Skulls served as water carriers. Coorong, S.A. 4, 5 - Bone awl with sheath found at Fromm's Landing, S.A. 6 - Possum jaw engraving tool, Vic. 7, 8 - Fromm's Landing archaeological excavation.

Trade and Exchange

The natural concentration of essential raw materials in restricted localities gave rise to trade and gift exchange which was an important aspect of Aboriginal economic, social and ritual life. Stone for implement production, woods and gums for weapons and utensils; ochre pigments for decorations; and many artifacts, ornaments and sacred objects, were exchanged and bartered along well-defined tracks.

Major trade routes criss-crossed the continent; Cape York in Queensland was connected by trade to southern Australia. Small sections of bailer-shells chipped and ground into ovate pieces were among the items that found their way down the river systems in the interior of eastern Australia to Cooper Creek, thence to Lake Eyre and on to the ochre and grindstone quarries in the Flinders Ranges. These items were ascribed great significance and used in sorcery as well as being incorporated into the most sacred rituals. This north-south route continued on to Port Augusta, down Spencer and St. Vincent gulfs, to Lake Alexandrina and the Coorong, finally reaching the mouth of the Glenelg River in western Victoria.

Another important trade route commenced on the north-west coast of Western Australia where pearl-shells shaped into pendants and often incised on the inner side with patterns, were traded to many parts of the interior, some travelling over 1500 kilometres from their place of origin.

Different types of stone found their way to regions where good quality material was in short supply. Axe-heads from an extensive quarry at Mt. William in Victoria reached South Australia and New South Wales; others from quarries in Queensland were traded down the river systems to Lake Eyre and central Australia.

Ochre pigments, used regularly for body decorations and the painting of artifacts, were traded widely from a limited number of deposits. Groups of Aboriginals made expeditions from western Queensland to obtain highly prized iridescent ochre mined in the Flinders Ranges of South Australia. Beanwood shields were the principal item received in exchange by the owners of the ochre source.

Boomerangs made in central Australia and the Northern Territory were traded extensively; Arnhem Land groups, who did not make them, secured these weapons in this way for use as musical clap-sticks.

The stems and leaves of the narcotic called 'pitcheri' (*Duboisia hopwoodii*) and other similar narcotics growing in south-west Queensland and central Australia, were dried, broken into small pieces and bartered in special bags. Pitcheri was ground into fragments and mixed with ashes before being chewed for its mild narcotic effect.

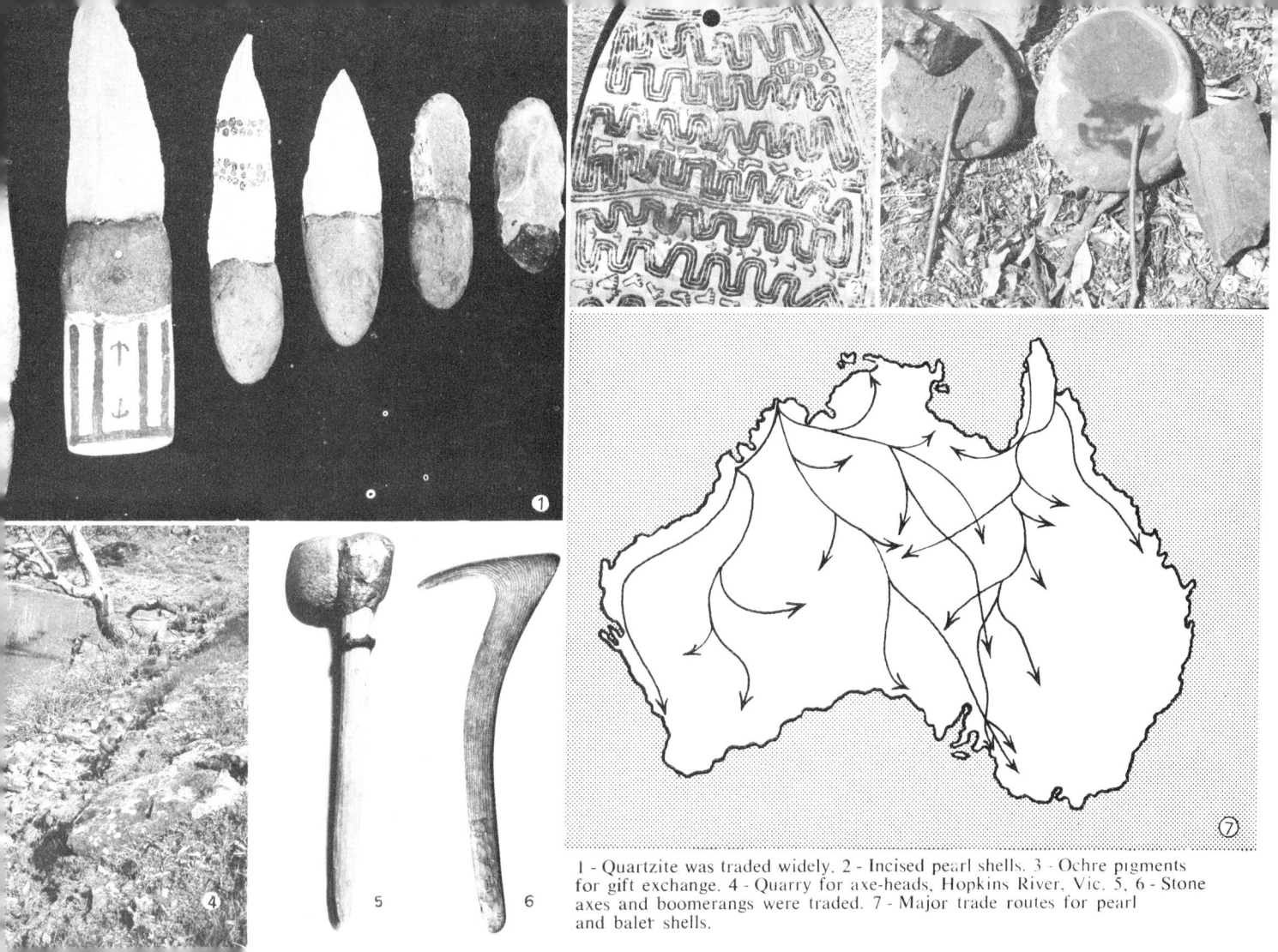

1 - Quartzite was traded widely. 2 - Incised pearl shells. 3 - Ochre pigments for gift exchange. 4 - Quarry for axe-heads, Hopkins River, Vic. 5, 6 - Stone axes and boomerangs were traded. 7 - Major trade routes for pearl and balet shells.

Rock Engravings

The art of abrading, pecking and hammering designs into the surface of rocks was a tradition carried out in most parts of Australia over a long period of time.

Aboriginal rock engravings were found first in Australia in the Sydney-Hawkesbury district of New South Wales by some of the immigrants who arrived with the First Fleet in 1788. Concentrated on comparatively flat rock surfaces, the designs they discovered were large and impressive and depicted men and women, mammals, birds, reptiles and fish often grouped with circles, weapons, ornaments, utensils and implements.

The engravings were made by scratching the outline of the subject on the rock surface and then making a series of overlapping punctures or pits to form a continuous groove which was gradually widened and deepened by rubbing during rituals. Most of the engravings are life-sized, but there are many unusually large examples; huge kangaroos up to seven metres high, koalas near two metres, emus five metres, human forms of ten metres and whales eighteen metres long.

The earliest known art was found in total darkness, deep inside Koonalda Cave on the Nullarbor Plain in South Australia. Here, extensive areas of wall markings 20,000 years old were made by artists who drew their fingers over the talc-like surface of the cave walls or cut grooves into the more consolidated rock.

The pecking technique of engraving animals and their tracks, geometric motifs and a range of abstract symbols on rock surfaces occurs widely in all states except Victoria. The sites are situated near springs, soakages, rockholes and other water supplies. At some sites such as Mootwingee in western New South Wales, there are many finely engraved silhouettes of men and animals. Some of the most exciting finds have been made in the remote Cleland Hills of central Australia where prehistoric engravings of human faces have added new designs to the known record of Aboriginal art.

Dateable engravings between 5,000 and 7,000 years old were discovered in an excavation at Ingaladdi on Willeroo Station nearly 160 kilometres south-west of Katherine in the Northern Territory. Several fragments of rock with abraded grooves and kangaroo and emu tracks were found buried in occupation deposit. The fragments are badly weathered and the designs incomplete, suggesting that they were originally pecked or abraded into the cliffs above and were dislodged after many years of weathering.

North-western Australia is another region rich in rock engravings. Strangely distorted human figures and engravings of animals and geometric motifs occur in thousands. Outstanding galleries have been recorded throughout the Pilbara district.

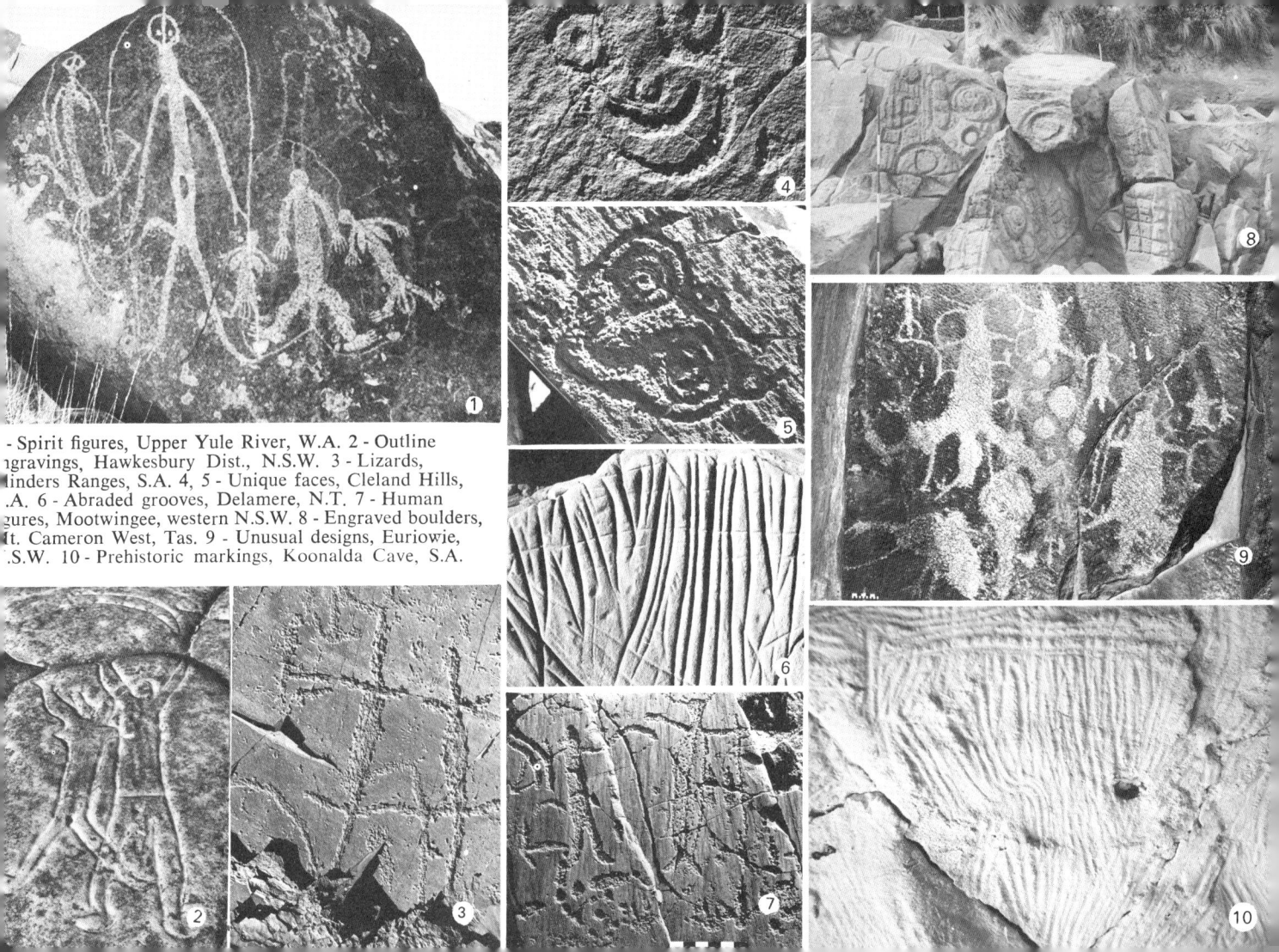

1 - Spirit figures, Upper Yule River, W.A. 2 - Outline engravings, Hawkesbury Dist., N.S.W. 3 - Lizards, Flinders Ranges, S.A. 4, 5 - Unique faces, Cleland Hills, N.A. 6 - Abraded grooves, Delamere, N.T. 7 - Human figures, Mootwingee, western N.S.W. 8 - Engraved boulders, Mt. Cameron West, Tas. 9 - Unusual designs, Euriowie, N.S.W. 10 - Prehistoric markings, Koonalda Cave, S.A.

Cave Paintings

Art is an important and integral part of Australian Aboriginal culture. Essentially the concern of the men, they painted in a wide range of styles from the elaborate 'X-ray' paintings found in the great rock shelters of western Arnhem Land to the simple line, track and geometric motifs of the centre.

The large and mouthless figures of the Wandjina art of the Kimberley Region of Western Australia are very distinctive. In western New South Wales there are concentrations of small human figures while in the galleries of Cape York the Aboriginal portrayed his totemic ancestors by large elaborate figures of man and animal. Outstanding too are the paintings of the great mythical creator, Nargorkun, situated in the galleries of the upper South Alligator River region of Arnhem Land. According to Aboriginal lore this legendary hero caused the ground to crack, fire to emerge, and forced rocks and ridges up to their present position.

Stencils are widely distributed in Australian cave art. Hands are common but there are also examples of stencilled human and animal feet and a range of weapons. Some of the best examples of this art style are found in the Carnarvon Ranges of central Queensland.

In some places it is still possible to study cave art with the aid of Aboriginals who regard it as a normal cultural expression. In Central Australia the Walbiri rituals associated with the Ngama and Ruguri cave painting sites play a significant role in what survives of tribal ceremonial life.

In the traditional situation the degree of sanctity varied from group to group. The drawing or redrawing of the figure of a mythical ancestor was usually intended to have some effect, direct or indirect, on their physical or spiritual environment. There were instances when individuals painted simply to pass the time, but over a wide area the act of painting, the finished product, and the associated ritual had magical and religious significance in the culture.

Despite the perishability of cave art, which demanded regular retouching for its preservation, it has been possible to look back some way into its past. In particular the art of central Australia had a code of rigid adherence to designs ordained by totemic ancestors at the time of creation of the Aboriginal world. In northern Australia the situation is in direct contrast. Here elaborate and colourful paintings, some showing undoubted Macassan influence, overlie art of a much simpler style.

In some regions the Aboriginals recorded in their galleries the first contacts with Europeans. There are many compositions featuring the white man with his guns and unusual animals.

The pigments used for painting were naturally occurring clays and rocks. Some groups were fortunate to have rich deposits in their own territory but others had to obtain supplies by trade or make long journeys to known sites. Pipeclay and gypsum served as a source of white colouring; limonite oxide, the dust inside ants' nests and sometimes fungus, were exploited as sources of yellow; black was obtained mainly from charcoal; red, the principal colour used, was derived from a large number of rocks and clays.

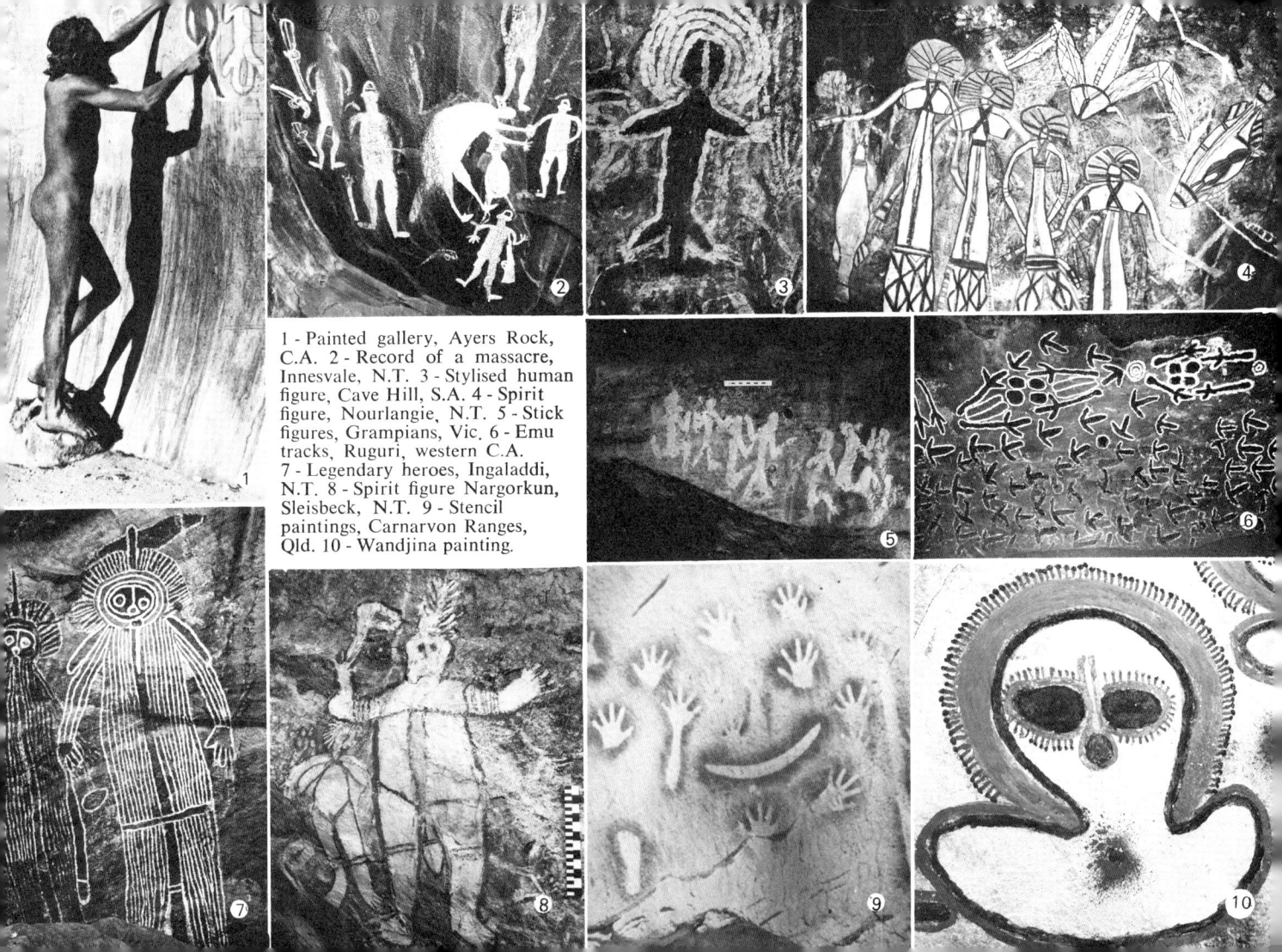

1 - Painted gallery, Ayers Rock, C.A. 2 - Record of a massacre, Innesvale, N.T. 3 - Stylised human figure, Cave Hill, S.A. 4 - Spirit figure, Nourlangie, N.T. 5 - Stick figures, Grampians, Vic. 6 - Emu tracks, Ruguri, western C.A. 7 - Legendary heroes, Ingaladdi, N.T. 8 - Spirit figure Nargorkun, Sleisbeck, N.T. 9 - Stencil paintings, Carnarvon Ranges, Qld. 10 - Wandjina painting.

Bark Paintings

There is a belief that bark painting began when the people of northern Australia whiled away the enforced idleness of the wet season by decorating the interior of their wet weather shelters.

There is little sophistication in the few materials used for a bark painting — a sheet of bark, a few basic pigments, some vegetable fixative and three or four twig brushes. The selection of these essentials was often a prolonged task as suitable materials were sometimes difficult to find and had to be obtained by trade.

The paintings reveal a keen appreciation of personal artistic expression among the Arnhem Land Aboriginals. The Aboriginal artist had definite restrictions on what he could paint, especially where sacred designs were concerned. Painted barks which featured in sacred ritual were stored in specially constructed shelters on ceremonial grounds. Their use in ceremonies was similar to that of other forms of artistic expression such as body painting, ceremonial spears, clubs and other objects.

In non-religious painting the artist chose designs and themes which belonged to him by virtue of membership of a particular kinship or totemic group. Often a whole legendary story was told on a single bark.

In eastern Arnhem Land the paintings consist of remarkable compositions which cover the whole surface of the bark. They incorporate totemic animals and plants; ancestral beings, including many snakes; and also clouds, rain, waves and other natural features of the land, sea and sky. Some of the designs are sacred, others are simply pictures of hunting and fishing grounds, mortuary rites, camp dances, Macassan boats, and daily activities.

In western Arnhem Land the majority of the paintings are elaborate 'X-ray' figures in a plain field. They are used for sorcery and for hunting, fishing and love magic and often depict totemic animals and mythical creatures.

On Groote Eylandt totemic animals are depicted as single figures, and there are compositions illustrating the lives of spiritual ancestors and the mythology of the sky-world which are painted on a black, yellow or red field.

The people of Melville and Bathurst Islands have a strong tradition for brightly coloured, highly abstract designs having mythological significance.

An outstanding collection of bark paintings was made at Oenpelli in 1912 by pioneer Australian anthropologist Sir Baldwin Spencer. This fine series of barks is now displayed in the National Museum of Victoria.

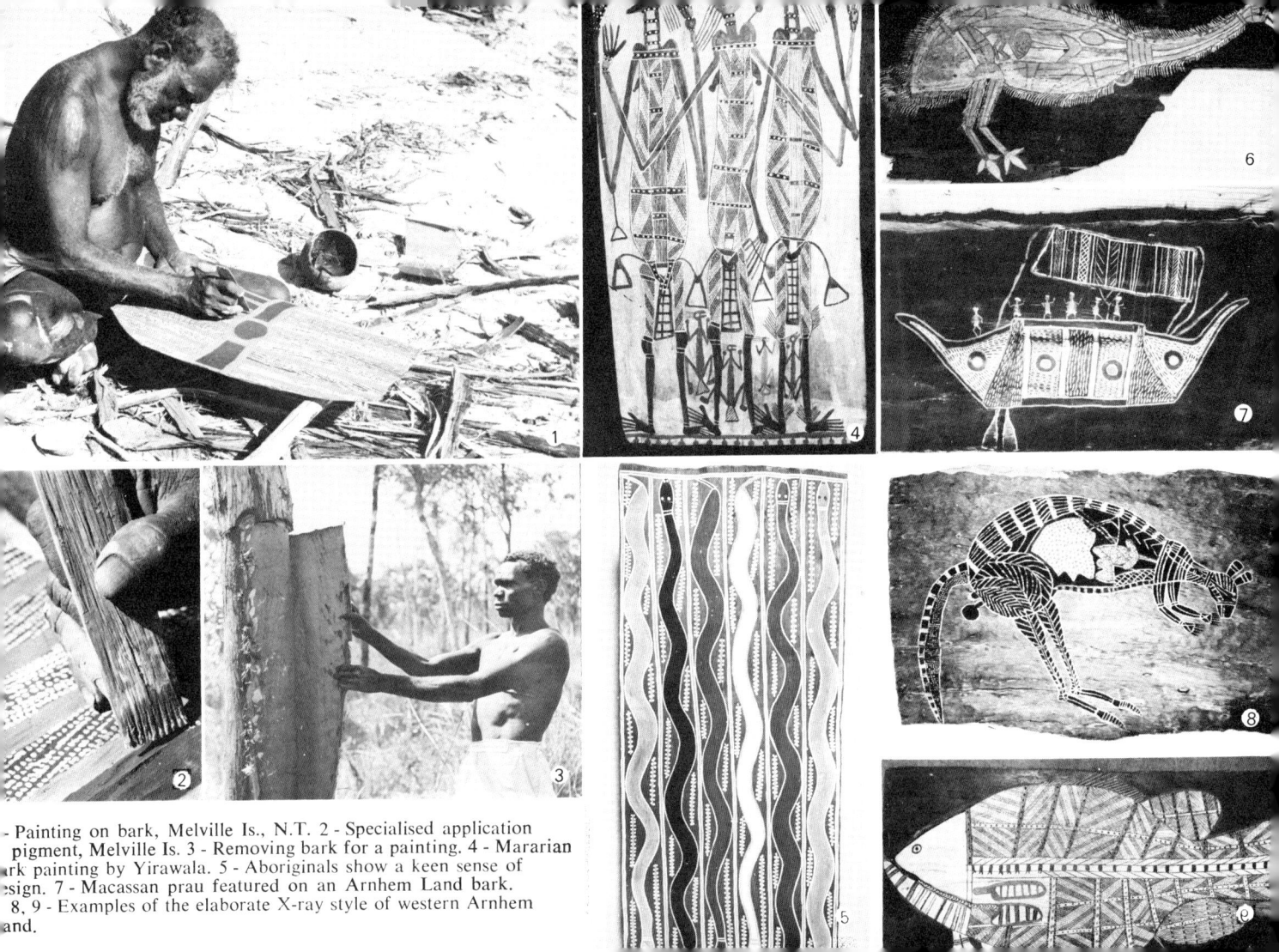

- Painting on bark, Melville Is., N.T. 2 - Specialised application
 pigment, Melville Is. 3 - Removing bark for a painting. 4 - Mararian
rk painting by Yirawala. 5 - Aboriginals show a keen sense of
sign. 7 - Macassan prau featured on an Arnhem Land bark.
 8, 9 - Examples of the elaborate X-ray style of western Arnhem
 and.

Old Age and Death

Old people were well cared for by the family and respected for their old age, wisdom and knowledge of tribal lore.

Mourning customs varied from region to region, but always included frantic displays of sorrow and distress. All cried and wailed in the most mournful manner; the women smeared themselves with white ochre, scratched their faces and bodies and beat one another about the head with clubs, while the men cut deep wounds in their thighs with stone knives.

Burial rites and modes of disposing of the dead were complex and varied, with their main purpose to ensure the safe return of the spirits of the dead to the spirit home or totemic centre by way of a water-hole, the sky or some offshore island. The rites also safe-guarded the living from the spirit's displeasure and served to avenge the deceased.

Rites were performed often at the grave or exposure-platform of the dead to discover the person to be blamed for the 'murder', since death was not considered a natural event and cause for it was always sought in the evil intentions of someone else, usually a member of another local group.

Different methods of disposing of the dead were practised in Australia. Simple disposal included abandonment, cremation, burial in the ground or in trees, placing on free-standing platforms, and deposition in caves and rock shelters. More complex disposals involved prolonged ritual. Often after the remains had decayed they were recovered and burnt, buried, placed in a log coffin, a cave, a rock shelter, a hollow tree, or the branches of a tree. Sometimes relics of the dead, such as a mummified hand or a red ochre smeared fore-arm bone, were kept as a memorial for long periods after the final disposal of the major part of the remains.

The ceremony of the *Pukamani* burial ritual on Melville and Bathurst Islands was long and elaborate. Large groups gathered for the final rites. Dancers wore elaborate body decorations and mimed events in the life of the deceased person and other traditional rituals. Large carved and decorated poles were made over the preceding months and erected around the grave during the rites.

In the lower Murray River region of South Australia the bodies of young men killed in group fights were set up cross-legged with their weapons on a wooden platform. Fires kindled beneath the structure gradually dried the bodies while relatives and tribesmen sat in silent mourning. After the bodies had remained on the platform for several weeks they were taken down and buried.

Skeletal remains have been recovered in many archaeological excavations. The cremated remains of a young woman dated to 26,000 years old, were found at Lake Mungo in western New South Wales. The early date for this site is evidence that cremation, which was also practised in Tasmania, has a Pleistocene antiquity in Australia. This makes Australian cremation the oldest known example of this form of burial.

1 - The final rites, Melville Is., N.T. 2 - Painted skull, [Arn]hem Land. 3 - Gypsum widows' cap, Dieri Tribe, S.A. [4 - L]ifting corpse on to burial platform, N.T. 5 - Mourning [amul]et, MacDonnell Ranges, C.A. 6 - Pipe-clay rubbed [into] hair as sign of widowhood. 7 - Cremation of mummified [body], Archer River, Q/ld. 8 - Women embracing and [cry]ing after cutting their heads during mourning ceremony. [9 - A]boriginal grave, Innamincka, S.A.

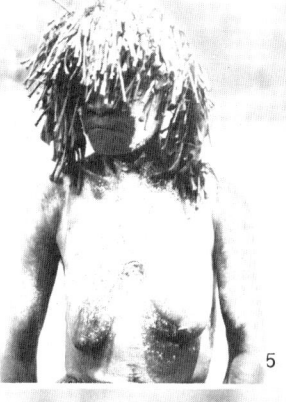

What of the Future?

Today Aboriginals live mainly in missions or settlements on outback reserves, on pastoral properties or in or near towns and cities. More than 350 separate reserves with a combined area of almost 550,000 square kilometres are set aside for their use. In remote parts of central and northern Australia Aboriginals continue to perform rituals make artifacts and live partly off the land, but continue also to adapt elements of European culture to their traditional life.

In the main, the culture of the Aboriginals described in this booklet has been brought to an end in the brief period of 200 years since Australia was discovered and settled by immigrants from Europe.

For many years the Aboriginals and their culture were ridiculed by the new arrivals and ruthless exploitation of the environment was pursued with little consideration for the people who had lived in complete harmony with the Australian landscape for many thousands of years. Lack of communication and understanding dominated relations with Aboriginals during this period and contributed to the degradation of a proud people and the total extinction of many groups.

Today attitudes are more enlightened and efforts are being made to ensure that the Aboriginal has a rightful place in the community. The Aboriginals face many difficulties as they grapple with a new and changing world. Generally they are notably less healthy, poorer, ill-housed and ill-educated compared with the rest of the population. Ill-health and low immunity to infectious diseases creates distress, inadequate housing leads to discontentment and lack of job opportunities causes frustration. These are but a few of the problems confronting a growing population of Aboriginals both in remote settlements and urban areas of Australia.

In a more enlightened age the pressures to abandon the 'old ways' have been to a large extent relaxed and many Aboriginals in distant parts of the continent enjoy something of the rich cultural life of traditional times. But it is difficult to preserve tangible relics of Aboriginal culture. With a lack of trained conservators a rich heritage of cave paintings, ancient rock engravings, stone arrangements, carved trees, stone and ochre quarries and other priceless sites is being lost. Hopefully, many sites and some aspects of this unique heritage will be preserved for all Australians.

It is hoped this booklet will stimulate interest in Aboriginal Australia and engender a curiosity about Aboriginal life which will lead readers to search for further information through reading, visits to museums and galleries, and participation in local societies formed to encourage interest in such matters.

1 - The older men are custodians of tribal law. 2 - Aboriginal potter at Bagot, N.T. 3 - *Darby* assisting in the South Australian Museum. 4, 5 - Aboriginal children have the benefit of education. 6 - Aboriginal stockman and family, Mainoru Station, N.T.

ACKNOWLEDGMENTS

Photographs were made available through the generosity of the following individuals and institutions:

Adelaide Advertiser: p. 47-3. Aiston, G. (S.A. Mus. Col.): p. 19-2: p. 29-2, 6: p. 31-4, 8: p. 45-3. Australian Museum: p. 11-9: p. 17-5: p. 25-5: p. 31-6. Basedow, H. (Aust. Inst. Anat. Col.): p. 3-7, 9: p. 7-7: p. 9-8: p. 11-3, 4: p. 13-1, 6, 7: p. 15-1: p. 21-2: p. 23-10: p. 25-3: p. 27-2, 4: p. 29-4: p. 45-4, 6, 9. Burnell, G. (S.A. State Lib. Col.): p. 25-8. Casey, D. A.: p. 5-6: p. 35-7, 8. Chilman, L.: p. 23-8. Crawford, I. M.: p. 41-10. Dix, W. C.: p. 39-1. Dunlop, I. (A.I.A.S. Col.): p. 3-5. Edwards, R.: p. 7-2, 5, 6, 8, 10: p. 9-3: p. 11-5, 6: p. 13-3, 8: p. 15-4 to 9: p. 17-6: p. 19-4, 5: p. 25-1: p. 29-7, 8: p. 33-1 to 6, 8: p. 35-4, 5: p. 37-2, 3, 5, 6: p. 39-3 to 10: p. 41-2 to 4, 6 to 8: p. 43-1 to 5, 8, 9: p. 45-2: p. 47-6. Elkin, A. P.: p. 27-1. Gillen, F. J. (S.A. Mus. Col.): p. 3-1, 6: p. 19-1, 3: p. 23-2: p. 29-3, 5: p. 35-1: p. 45-5. Hackett, C. J. (S.A. Mus. Col.): p. 9-1, 7: p. 15-2: p. 21-3. Kerry, C. (Tyrrell Col.): p. 17-4: p. 27-5. Love, J. R. B. (Brit. Mus. Col.): p. 5-2: p. 25-2. Macintosh, N. W. G.: p. 23-6. Maynard, L.: p. 39-2. McConnel, U. (S.A. Mus. Col.): p. 25-7: p. 27-3: p. 31-5, 7: p. 45-7. McKnight, C. C.: p. 25-4. Mountford, C. P. (S.A. State Lib. Col.): p. 3-8: p. 9-5: p. 11-2, 7: p. 15-3: p. 17-3, 7: p. 21-1, 9, 10: p. 31-1: p. 41-1: p. 45-1. Mulvaney, D. J.: p. 5-3, 4. Mumford, W.: p. 5-1. National Museum of Victoria: p. 35-6. Peterson, N. C. (A.I.A.S. Col.): p. 13-4, 5: p. 31-3. Pitt Rivers Museum (Oxford): p. 35-3. Roberts, A.: p. 7-1, 4, 9: p. 43-7. South Australian Museum: p. 3-2, 3, 4: p. 9-9: p. 27-6: p. 33-7: p. 41-9. Spencer, Baldwin (Nat. Mus. of Vic. Col.): p. 9-2, 6: p. 11-1, 8: p. 13-2: p. 19-6: p. 23-3, 7, 9: p. 31-2: p. 35-2: p. 43-6: p. 45-8. Stocker, E. O. (S.A. Mus. Col.): p. 27-7. Taplin, G. (S.A. Mus. Col.): p. 23-4, 5: p. 25-6. Thorne, A. G.: p. 5-5. Wallace, N. M.: p. 17-2: p. 47-4, 5: p. 48-1, 2. West, A. L.: p. 37-5: p. 41-5. Worrell, E.: p. 27-8.

Grateful thanks are recorded to the many colleagues who commented on the manuscript. Design and layout are by Mr Ainslie Roberts and cover design Miss Pat Marsden.

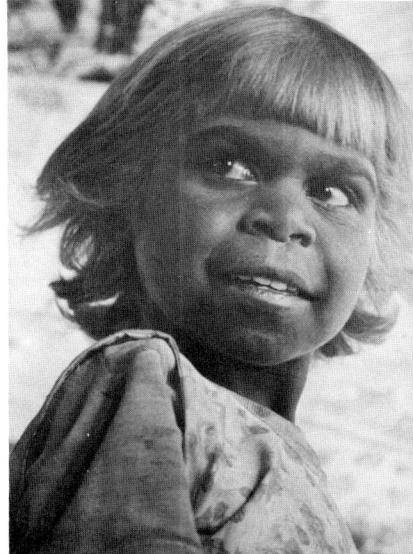

1 - *Kalykulya*, Everard, S.A.
2 - *Barbara*, Everard, S.A.

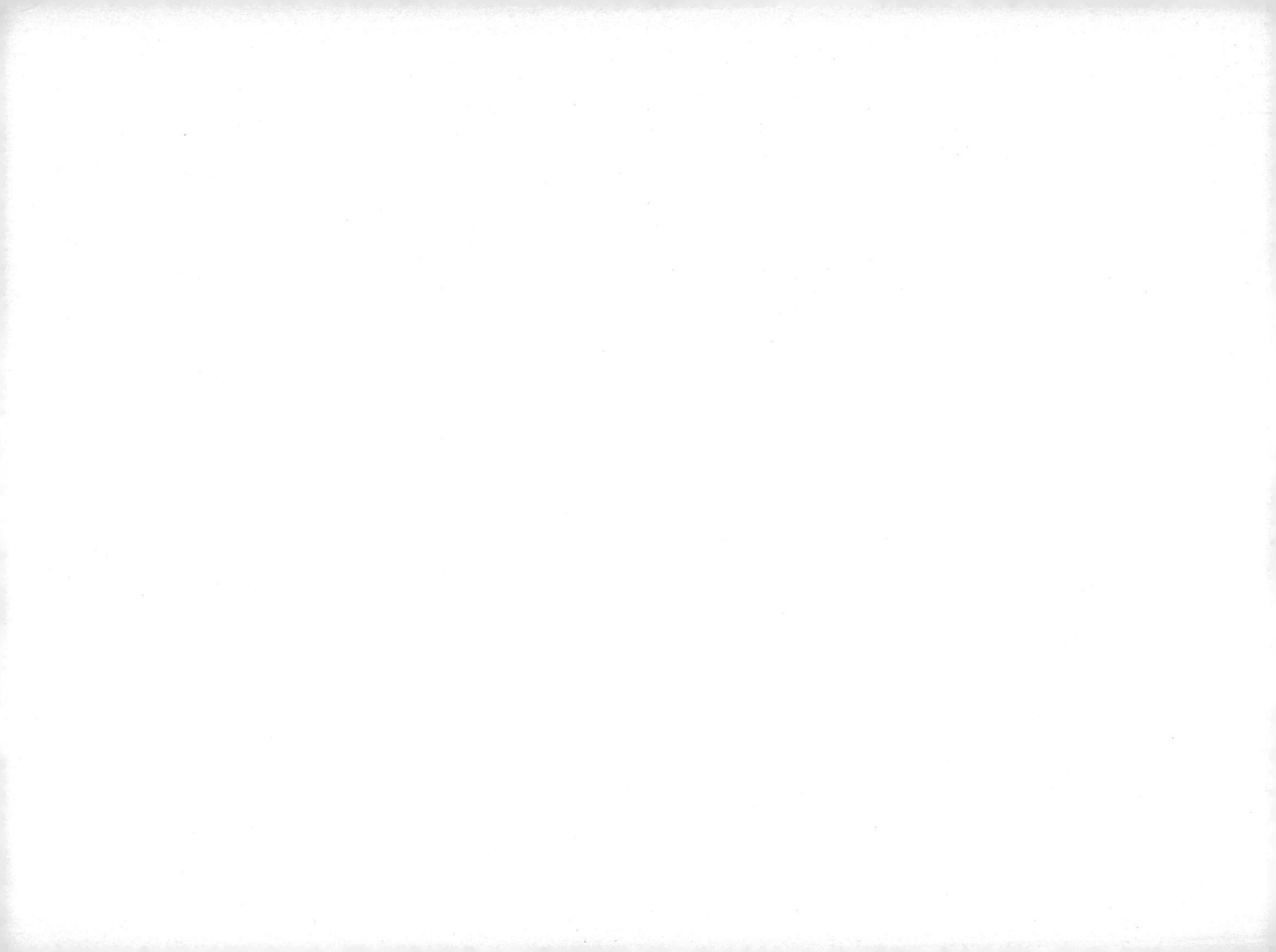